P9-DMY-183

Ethiopian Voices

Tsion's Life

AMHARIC
KIDS.COM

Stacy Bellward

photographs
Erlend Berge

These are photos of me when I was a baby and at my one-year birthday. Some people have a cake for their birthday, but most people in Ethiopia have a special bread called difo dabo.

Say "beautiful": konjo

My name is Tsion. I am eleven years old, and I live in the East African country of Ethiopia. Our capital city is Addis Ababa. I speak Amharic and a little English. Many Ethiopian names have a meaning. My name means "heaven," but my mom calls me Amarech, a name that means beautiful.

More than three million people live in Addis Ababa, but most Ethiopians live in the country. There are more than eighty languages spoken in Ethiopia. Amharic is written different from English. For example, "thank you" is written like this: አመሰግናለሁ. Each part of this book will teach you how to say a new word in Amharic.

Say "palace": bete mengest

I am proud of my country because of its long history, beautiful traditions, and special places. Someday I want to visit Lalibela, where eleven churches were carved out of a stone mountain and are connected by tunnels.

Lalibela is a blessed and holy place.

The city of Gondar in northern Ethiopia is called "the Camelot of Africa" because it has a palace, churches, bridges, and towers. The sunken stone bathing places are still used today.

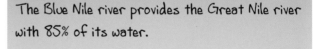

The Blue Nile river provides the Great Nile river with 85% of its water.

Say "family": bete seb

I live with my family and our housekeeper in the same house I've lived in my whole life. It's inside a compound with two other houses, and it has three rooms: a kitchen, a bedroom, and a living room. We share a bathroom and water tap with the other two houses. I visit my grandmother and great-grandmother a couple of times a week because they live together just down the street.

We collect and save water with these buckets.

Many families like Tsion's hire housekeepers from rural Ethiopia. Amsalech is sixteen years old, but she started working in Addis Ababa when she was eleven. She earns money by cleaning and cooking for Tsion's family. Amsalech sends some of the money back to her own family who lives in the country.

Say "town": ketema

We live in a part of Addis Ababa called Kechene. People here do not have much money, but instead of begging, they work hard. Some people earn money by making and selling handicrafts like traditional weaving and clay pottery. My uncle is a weaver and made me a beautiful, soft, white netella, which is a traditional headscarf.

Wundinesh is making clay pots that we will use for cooking, carrying water, and decorating our house.

The people in Kechene are kind and very friendly. Kechene is a poor area, and the people who live there only get water on two days each week: Wednesday and Sunday. They have electricity most of the time. Kechene is right next to the Entoto Mountains, which are the highest places in Addis Ababa.

Yigren is making thread that will be turned into a thick blanket-like shawl called a gabi. Gabis are like tennis shoes to Americans—everybody has them.

My father always tells me the most important things in life are to work hard and respect other people.

Say "father": abat

My father was a taxi driver, but it did not pay enough and he had to work too much. Now he is a butcher like my grandfather used to be. On two days each week, he drives a truck that carries butchered sheep and cows from the countryside into the city. When my father is not working, he likes to exercise by running to the Entoto Mountains.

Many of the people in Ethiopia are Ethiopian Orthodox Christian. It is against their religious tradition to sell meat on Wednesdays and Fridays. On those days, Tsion's father does not have to work. Someday he hopes to get an office job.

This is my parents' wedding in 1994.

Say "mother": enat

My mother wakes up at 6:30 every morning to make breakfast and help my brother and me get ready for school. She teaches me about God and tells me to be polite and kind to other people. My mother wants me to do well in school so that, someday, I can go to a university.

Tsion's mother works every day as a manager of a government-owned restaurant. In the afternoon, she has a couple of free hours to go home and cook or visit friends. She works again in the evenings and comes home at 10:00 at night.

My mother says I can be anything I want when I grow up, as long as I am kind and generous to others.

Say "brother": wundim

My brother, Yonas, is four years old. I nicknamed him Rebash, which means "pest," because when my friends visit, he bothers us. After school, I have to take care of Yonas. I worry that he will leave our compound and get hurt, so I watch him carefully to make sure he is safe.

Yonas was named after Jonah in the Bible. Tsion and Yonas love each other very much, but like all sisters and brothers, they argue. Sometimes Yonas kicks Tsion. She cries but never kicks him back because she is older.

I help Yonas wash himself by using a bowl and a pitcher of water. We wash ourselves in the yard outside our house.

My great-grandmother tells me to study hard, keep good friends, and obey my parents. I love her very much!

Say "grandmother": sayt ayat

I love my mother, grandmother, and great-grandmother. These are my favorite people! My great-grandmother is eighty-nine years old. She got married when she was only seven years old and had her first baby when she was thirteen years old. I can hardly believe that! She tells me true stories about her life.

Tsion's great-grandmother and grand mother earn money by selling meals from their home. They buy potatoes from the *merkato*, or outdoor market. They peel the potatoes, cook them, and then add oil, green peppers, chili peppers, and beetroot. People come to their home and pay about fifty cents to eat dinner. Age is highly respected in Ethiopia. Only 3 percent of Ethiopians are older than sixty-five.

Say "pray": selot

My family's religion is Ethiopian Orthodox Christianity. We sing songs and say prayers in the morning and at night before bed. We go to church a few times each week. Most Ethiopian Orthodox churches are octagon-shaped, which means they have eight sides. We have to take our shoes off before going in because it is a holy place.

I kiss the cross for an extra blessing.

About 45 percent of Ethiopians are members of the Orthodox Church. Members worship God and many angels and saints. On 165 days a year, including every Wednesday and Friday, Ethiopian Orthodox Christians only eat vegetables and bread and skip break-fast entirely.

Say "candy": karamella

Sometimes my mother asks me to go and buy things at a roadside shop called a gulit. I don't mind going, but when I buy tomatoes that are not ripe enough, my mother makes me go back and exchange them. I really don't like it when that happens, because I get so embarrassed when I have to face the shopkeeper again.

Everyday food such as fruit, oil, and eggs are sold at little stands along the road. The *merkato* in Addis Ababa is the biggest outdoor market in Africa. At smaller neighborhood markets, farmers come from the countryside with their donkeys to sell grains such as *tef*. Tef is used to make the Ethiopian bread called *injera*.

Whenever I have a little money,
I either give it to beggars or
buy chocolates and candy.

Say "school": temhert bet

I am in sixth grade. My favorite subject is astronomy because space and stars are so mysterious. My teacher tells me that space has no beginning and no end, but I can hardly believe that. I want to learn more about stars and discover what is in space. There has to be more to know, and I want to find out.

Tsion goes to a private school that costs twenty dollars a month. She walks thirty-five minutes to school and has thirty-nine students in her classroom. Half of the children in Ethiopia go to school.

I walk to school every day with Meron. She's one of my best friends.

We have been to Bora Amusement Park two times.
Last Christmas, I met Santa Claus there!

Say "friend": gwadenya

Mulualim, Tsedale, Rihana, and Meron are my best friends. We play singing and clapping games and volleyball together. When we play house, we use any bits and pieces we can find for pretend dishes and food. Yonas is always the baby. Sometimes I go and ask the clothes tailor down the street for fabric scraps, and then I make little dolls out of them.

Ethiopian children do not have many toys. Tsion has one doll and a stuffed toy dog. She does not like real cats or dogs, but she would like to have a pet monkey.

Say "food": megeb

My mother makes injera every three days. Injera is sour bread that looks like a huge, thick pancake. We eat it with almost every meal. There is a shed in our compound that is built especially for making injera. We put wat on the injera and also hold it with our fingers to scoop up food. Yum!

Ethiopia's national dish is *injera* and *wat*. Wat is a thick stew that is often very spicy. There are many types of meat and vegetable wat. It is always served on injera.

This grain is called tef. It is very healthy for our bodies, and it is the main ingredient of injera.

My favorite Ethiopian food is siga wat, which is made with meat. But I like hamburgers too.

Say "coffee": buna

We serve coffee when guests come to our house. The first time I helped, I burned my hand. I know how to make coffee, but there are three things I'm not very good at. First, I roast the beans until they are too dark. Second, I am not strong enough to really pound them into powder. Third, I get impatient and pour the coffee before it is ready. So now I just serve a snack called kolo with the coffee.

Coffee was first discovered by a shepherd boy in the Keffa hills of southwestern Ethiopia. Since then, the Ethiopian coffee ceremony has been an important part of welcoming guests. Each guest drinks at least three cups of coffee. It is said that the third cup brings a blessing.

We eat dinner in the living room at about 8:00 in the evening. On the days when we don't eat meat, a normal dinner includes injera, vegetables, and alitcha (mild) wat.

Say "night": mata

Before bedtime, I do my schoolwork and help Yonas with his schoolwork too. We also watch TV. I like cartoons and shows about Ethiopian history. If Yonas can't get to sleep, I sing him a song about Jesus or let him hold my doll. Before we sleep, we always say our prayers.

Tsion's parents sleep in the bedroom. Tsion and Yonas share the top of the bunk bed in the living room. Amsalech, the family's housekeeper, sleeps in the bottom bunk.

Bless my night
As you have blessed my day.
God, please help me
Sleep the night in peace.
Amen

Meet Tsion (SEE yon) via video clip, and hear audio pronunciations of the Amharic words in this book at www.amharickids.com.

Pronunciation

There is no standard for transliterating Amharic, or putting it into Roman characters. Familiarize yourself with how the vowels are used below. All r's are rolled.

u	gut, bud
oo	shoot, choose
ee	free, tea
a	sad, mat
ay	cake, safe, hay
i	evil, dish
o	go, show

Published by Amharic Kids
7201 88th Avenue North
Brooklyn Park, Minnesota 55445
www.amharickids.com
info@amharickids.com

Thank you Tsion and family for being Ethiopian ambassadors. Solomon Bogale, your assistance as an interpreter and cultural guide is greatly appreciated. Kate, I could not have done without your expertise and encouragement. Aster, thank you for patiently answering all my questions about Ethiopia and for your Amharic expertise.

Library of Congress Control Number: 2008904247
ISBN: 978-0-9797481-1-0
Printed in Minnesota

AMHARIC KIDS.COM

For all of us who wonder what life might have been like in Ethiopia. And for my beautiful girls- I can't wait to travel the world with you.

Stacy spent her teenage years in Tanzania, and although she has lived and worked on four continents, she holds Ethiopia especially close since adopting their Ethiopian-born daughter. In response to the lack of Ethiopian resources for adoptive families, she wrote her first book, *Our First Amharic Words*. Together with her husband, Paul, she launched Amharic Kids. Stacy and Paul live with their two daughters in Minnesota but look forward to the day when they can spend extended time giving back in Ethiopia.

Erlend Berge, a freelance journalist and photographer from Norway, has traveled through many countries for work and pleasure—always with a camera. He recently had "four fantastic months in Ethiopia, enjoying great food, the best coffee, and the famous Ethiopian hospitality." His works include a black-and-white photography book entitled *Moments from Nepal* and many photographs and articles published in magazines and newspapers. Visit his Web site at www.erlendberge.no.